STETSON BRANCH
200 DIXWELL AVENUE
NEW HAVEN, CT 06511

MEAN MACHINES

MOTORBIKES

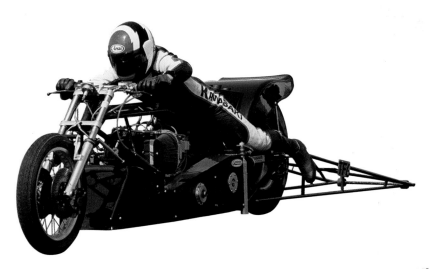

MARK MORRIS

Chicago, Illinois

© 2005 Raintree
Published by Raintree,
A division of Reed Elsevier, Inc.
Chicago, IL

All rights reserved. No part of this publication may be reproduced or transmitted in any form or by any means, electronic or mechanical, including photography, recording, taping, or any information storage and retrieval system, without permission in writing from the publishers.

For information, address the publisher:
Raintree, 100 N. LaSalle, Suite 1200, Chicago, IL 60602

Customer Service: 888-363-4266
Visit our website at www.raintreelibrary.com

Printed and bound in China by South China Printing Company.
09 08 07 06 05
10 9 8 7 6 5 4 3 2 1

Library of Congress Cataloging-in-Publication Data:

Morris, Mark, 1965-
  Motorbikes / Mark Morris.
     p. cm. -- (Mean machines)
  Includes bibliographical references and index.
  ISBN 1-4109-0558-6 (library binding, hardcover) -- ISBN 1-4109-0832-1 (pbk.) 1. Minibikes--Juvenile
literature. I. Title. II. Series.
  TL443.M67 2004
  629.227'5--dc22
                              2004014135

Acknowledgments
Alamy p.42; Alvey and Towers pp. 14, 24, 33, 49, 52; Andrew Morland pp. 7, 10, 17, 18; BMW p.32;
Car Photo Library pp. 25, 26, 28; Corbis pp. 7b (Bettman), 8, 20 (Roger Ressmeyer), 44 (top), 44 (bot)
(Bettman), 47 (Patrick Ward), 48 (Adam Woolfit), 50 (Bettman), 57; Dave Campos p.44; Dorling Kindersley
p.11; Ducati p.6; Empics pp. 31, 32, 34–35, 36, 37, 38, 40 (bot); Eye Ubiquitous p.43 (Darren Maybury); Giles
Chapman pp. 54, 56; Harley Davidson pp. 16 (bot), 29 (bot); Honda pp. 16 (bot), 30, 46, 54; Mirrorpix pp. 4,
22, 22, 23, 35, 52, 55; National Motor Museum, Beaulieu pp. 8, 10, 45; PA Photos pp. 38, 39, 50; Phoenix
Distribution p.21; Rex Features pp. 19, 51; Ron Kimball Studios p.53; Sporting Pitcures p.41; Suzuki pp. 14, 15,
24, 37, 46; Sylvia Cordaiy p.32–33; Topfoto pp. 6, 12, 30, 34, 36, 40 (top), 42, 48, 56; TRH Pictures pp. 12, 13,
29; Triumph Motorcycles pp. 20, 27; Triumph p.18–19.

Cover photograph of a Kawasaki Ninja reproduced with permission of Action Plus.

Every effort has been made to contact copyright holders of any material reproduced in this book. Any omissions will
be rectified in subsequent printings if notice is given to the publisher.

Disclaimer
All the Internet addresses (URLs) given in this book were valid at the time of going to press. However, due to the
dynamic nature of the Internet, some addresses may have changed, or sites may have changed or ceased to exist
since publication. While the author and publisher regret any inconvenience this may cause readers, no
responsibility for any such changes can be accepted by either the author or the publisher.

CONTENTS

Any words appearing in the text in bold,
like this, are explained in the glossary.
You can also look out for them in the "Up to
Speed" box at the bottom of each page.

THE BEST BIKES

This book is not about ordinary motorcycles. It is about the best. The motorcycles that beat the rest.

The best bikes do things that others cannot. A racing motorbike can **accelerate** like a rocket and fly around corners at incredible speeds. An off-road motorcycle can handle difficult conditions and jump over obstacles. Then there are **production motorcycles**. These are superbikes designed to **perform** like track racers, but any member of the public can buy one.

There are also the motorcycles that just want to go faster and faster. Some are specially built to break records. Others take part in drag races.

CRUISER

Bikes like the Harley-Davidson Road King **cruiser** have an old-fashioned design. They are just as much about image and style as **performance**.

A Harley-Davidson FLHR Road King.

cruiser   motorcycle built for comfort, looks, and style
limited edition   when only a small number are built

TREMENDOUS TWO-WHEELERS

You can see great bikes on the streets and you can hear them, too! You could go to a race track to see professionals racing these powerful machines to their limits.

There are a lot of bike shows where you can see awesome motorcycles. There are competitions for the best bikes and sometimes there are display shows, too.

There are even motorcycles in museums. Especially if they were a **limited edition** design or held a speed record.

Wherever you see them, one thing is for sure. Motorcycles are exciting. You get a thrill just from looking at them.

This bike holds the land-speed record for motorcycles.

FIND OUT LATER...

Which bikes have races that are over in seconds?

How are bikes used by the army?

Which bike has a roof?

perform / performance   how well a bike does things
production motorcycles   bikes built in large numbers

THE CYCLE STORY

There are different kinds of motorcycle for different styles of riding. Touring bikes are designed to be comfortable on long journeys. Off-road bikes are designed for fun on dirt tracks. **Cruisers** are designed for low-speed travel around town.

INDIAN HENDEE SPECIAL

This 1914 Indian Hendee Special was the first bike to have an electric motor. It only cost $325 to buy. Fewer than seven are still known to exist today.

Then there are the "superbikes." With superbikes, **performance** is the only thing that matters. Superbikes are built to be thrilling. Their weight, size, and power are carefully balanced to give maximum performance and excitement.

TECH TALK

Ducati 998s: technical data
- Engine size: 998 cc
- Engine type: L twin **cylinder**
- Engine power: 123 **bhp**
- Top speed: 165 mph (265.6 km/h)
- Weight: 437 lbs (198 kg)

cc (cubic centimeter) number that measures the size of an engine's cylinders. A higher number means a larger engine.

Riding a superbike means being out on the edge. They ride low to the ground and at very high speeds. They are the machines for speed freaks.

High-performance sports bikes are built to look like racing machines. They move so quickly thanks to a balance of weight and power. The lighter a bike is, the less engine power is needed to make it go. Lightweight bikes with very powerful engines can be difficult to control, however.

There are also many different sorts of racing competitions. Some races use specially built machines, others use **production motorcycles**.

SUZUKI RGV500

The Suzuki RGV500 has a 500 **cc** engine but weighs only 287 lbs. That is about 66-88 lbs. lighter than most 500 cc bikes. As a result it has been a successful racing bike and can reach speeds of 185 mph (296 km/h).

A Suzuki RGV500.

cylinder   tube-shaped part of an engine, where fuel is burned

bhp   rate at which an engine does work

THE FIRST POWERED BIKES

The very first motorcycles were built in the mid-1800s. They used steam engines to power them. These engines needed to burn wood or coal to make them go. Wood and coal are very heavy, and the engines took a long time to warm up. Steam-bikes belched out thick black smoke and had a dangerous habit of exploding!

By the 1880s gas engines were being used to power bikes. They were much better because they were ready to ride as soon as the engine started.

The first motorcycles went on sale in the early 1900s. They were ordinary pedal bikes with small engines bolted on to them.

DAIMLER

In 1885 Gottlieb Daimler built one of the first coal-powered motorcycles. His son Paul rode it for 8 miles (13 km) at a top speed of 10 mph (16 km/h). Unfortunately, Paul had to get off rather quickly when the bike burst into flames.

TECH TALK

The 1901 Werner was the first motorcycle to have its engine in the place we expect to find it today.

reputation   being well known for something

EARLY MOTORCYCLES

By 1914 real motorcycles were being built. Rather than attaching tiny gas engines to pedal bikes, companies could see that the motorbike had a future.

Motorcycles built by the company "Indian" were very popular. George Hendee and Oscar Hedstrom started the company in Springfield, Massachusetts. The company soon gained a **reputation** for good design and high quality.

Soon other companies were building bikes. They came in all shapes and sizes. Slowly they began to look more like those we see on the roads today.

THE WORLD'S FIRST

The 1894 Hildebrand and Wolfmuller Motorrad was the world's first **production motorcycle**. It was difficult to start and even harder to ride. But it was the first!

The 1894 Hildebrand and Wolfmuller had a top speed of 28 mph (45 km/h).

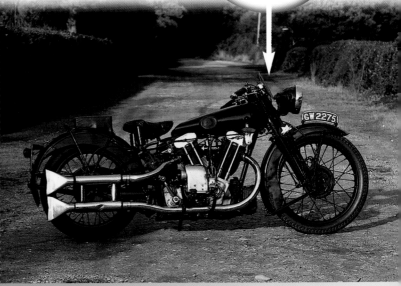

BETWEEN THE WARS

The 1920s were the **golden age** of motorcycling. Between the two World Wars, the motorcycle was more popular than at any other time.

After World War I finished in 1918, soldiers returned home. Many had used motor vehicles for the first time during the war. They now wanted to own one themselves.

To begin with the army sold off used motorcycles it no longer needed. This supply soon ran out. Businesspeople realized there was money to be made. Factories that had been producing guns, bullets, and tanks during the war were soon producing motorcycles.

By 1919 more than 50 new companies were building motorcycles. By 1921 the number had risen to 100.

Many once-famous manufacturers have now gone out of business.

The Brough Superior became very collectible after its use in the 1962 film, *Lawrence of Arabia.*

VINTAGE BIKES

Many famous motorbike brands disappeared in the 1920s and 1930s. Only bikes built before 1930 can really be called **vintage** motorcycles.

golden age   great period in history
sidecar   small car attached to the side of a motorbike

BIKES FOR EVERYONE

Motorcycles were everywhere in the 1920s. They were used for everyday transportation, work, and fun. **Sidecars** were built with enough seats for whole families. Butchers and bakers used specially designed motorcycles for making deliveries.

CARS OVERTAKE

By the end of the decade things were changing. Small cars were challenging the motorcycle. Cars had become cheap enough for most people.

Before long many famous motorcycle names had disappeared. Sunbeam, Douglas, and AJS were among the famous companies that went out of business. By World War II the golden age of motorcycling was over.

BROUGH SUPERIOR

The Brough Superior was the first great motrcycle built for speed. In its day it was called the Rolls-Royce of motorbikes. It was made between 1924 and 1939 and could go more than 100 mph (160 km/h).

The engine of the Brough Superior.

vintage   old, usually built between 1919 and 1930

MILITARY MOTORCYCLES

Motorcycles have been used in war for as long as aircraft. About 20,000 motorcycles were used in World War I. By the end of World War I in 1918, Harley-Davidson was selling half the bikes it made to the army.

A bike has many advantages in a war zone. It is:
- small
- cheap to run
- fast
- easy to pack into crates
- easy to drop from an aircraft.

Perhaps the biggest advantage is that a bike keeps going when the road does not. Bikes do many different jobs in a war, from carrying messages to attacking the enemy.

GERMAN BIKES

This BMW R75 bike was commonly used by German forces during World War II. Originally designed for use in the desert, it was good enough to **perform** well in any conditions. The **sidecar** usually had a machine-gun built on to it.

A Special Forces trailbike.

military   to do with the armed forces

ARMY BIKES TODAY

Today's **military** bikes have to cope with many different conditions. Bikes have been used in desert situations such as the 1991 Gulf War and the 2003 war in Iraq.

Military bikes are built to very high standards. They have to cope with sand clogging up their engines. The army had to find a way to make bikes run on diesel instead of regular gas because all other military vehicles use this fuel.

TECH TALK

In World War II the German army used new tactics to move fast. Motorcycles meant the army could move and attack very quickly.

FLYING FLEA

The Royal Enfield Flying Flea was a tiny 125 **cc** British bike. It was designed in 1940 for use in World War II. It was light enough to be dropped by parachute and carried by hand.

DESIGN TECHNOLOGY

Modern motorcycles have many different working parts. They are very different from the first motorcycles that appeared about 100 years ago. They are carefully designed and put together. They use the most up-to-date technology.

SIMPLER TIMES

Early motorcycles, such as the Norton Dominator above, were not very complicated. They were not very comfortable or efficient, either. There was no key to start the bike and signals were often given by hand.

LESS GIVES YOU MORE

One of the main differences between a modern motorcycle and its older relatives is the number of **integral parts**. This means more things are built all together on modern bikes. They are not built separately, then bolted to one another.

A modern bike with fewer separate parts is lighter and easier to take care of.

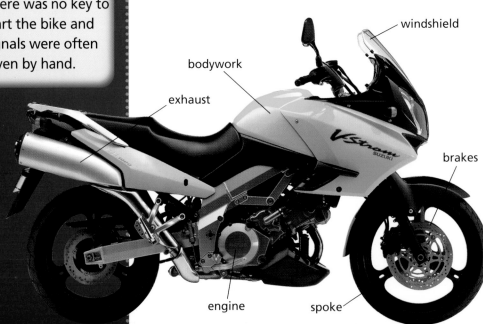

windshield

bodywork

exhaust

brakes

engine

spoke

integral parts   parts of a motorcycle built in a single piece, instead of joining several pieces together

NEW TECHNOLOGY

Less weight means more speed. Lightweight metals such as aluminum and titanium are used to build the engine. Many **components** are glued together with super-strong **bonding** materials. This is better than the old way of **welding**, which adds weight to the machine.

The bodywork is made of strong, lightweight plastic. The metal wheels have thinner walls and fewer **spokes**. All these developments help to improve the bike's **performance**.

As time goes by, motorcycles look less and less like the early versions. However, the thrill and fun of riding on two wheels is still the same.

SHOCK ABSORBERS

Shock absorbers above the wheels have two main parts: a steel spring and a **piston** connected to it. The spring absorbs the bumps as the bike travels. The piston moves inside a tube that is filled with gas, liquid, or air.

The suspension system on a motorcycle.

spoke   metal rod that runs from the center of a wheel to the outside edge

ENGINE TYPES

There are two main groups of cycle engine: **two-stroke** and **four-stroke**.

Engines have one or more **pistons**, which move up and down inside **cylinders**. They are powered by a mixture of gasoline and air. This mixture is exploded by a spark from the **spark plug**.

A four-stroke engine pushes the piston up and down four times after each spark. A two-stroke pushes twice. The pistons are connected to the **crankshaft**. The up-and-down motion is turned into a circular one. This motion is then **transmitted** to a chain, belt, or shaft that turns the back wheel.

A V-Twin engine.

An in-line four engine.

V-TWIN ENGINES

V-Twin engines power many machines. The two cylinders are set at an angle to each other. This makes the V-shape. These engines make a deep, rumbling noise that sounds very powerful. They are used to power Ducatis and Harley-Davidsons.

crankshaft   part of an engine that is joined to the pistons
spark plug   part of an engine that makes an electrical spark

ENGINE NAMES

Engines often get their names from how the cylinders are arranged. Usually more cylinders mean less engine **vibration** and noise. This makes the ride smoother. There are many different ways that cylinders can be arranged. Each way has advantages and disadvantages.

Most engines have cylinders that stand up. If they lie down, the engine is "flat." The Honda Gold Wing is powered by a flat-six. This means that the bike has a six-cylinder engine, with the cylinders lying flat.

The Suzuki RG500 uses a square-four. This engine has four cylinders that stand up in a square. The Yamaha YZF-R1's engine is an in-line-four. The four cylinders stand in a line inside the engine.

BOXER: THE FLAT TWIN

Originally designed in 1912, this classic flat-twin engine has been used by Porsche, Volkswagen, and Harley-Davidson. BMW began to use it in 1922 and it became a legend. A modern version of the Boxer is still in use today.

A Boxer flat-twin engine.

PRODUCTION MOTORCYCLES

Building a **production motorcycle** is a complicated job. A **production line** has to be set up. All the different parts have to arrive at the production line at the correct time.

Not all of the parts of a motorcycle are made by the same people. Parts from other factories are delivered to the production line. The bike moves slowly along the line where the **component** parts are added. Every single component is checked and tested before it is ready to use.

It is important to make sure everything runs smoothly. One missing part holds up the whole line. If the production line stops moving, the bike maker loses money.

SAFETY CHECKS

When a bike rolls off the end of a production line it is checked and tested many times. When it has passed every test, it is given a safety certificate. Only then can it be sold.

A production motorcycle is made up of parts from many different places.

automatically   on its own, without a person working it

MOVING ON

As the bike moves **automatically** along the production line, robot mechanics and skilled humans do different jobs. Eventually the completed bike arrives at the end of the line, ready for a test ride.

New motorcycles are packed into crates and sent all over the world to local dealers. People can look at them in the showroom and decide which one to buy.

TOP TECHNOLOGY

The latest technology is used in factories to build aproduction motorcycle. Computer technology and robots help to assemble the motorbikes very accurately.

This motorcycle is near the end of the production line. It is almost ready to be crated, shipped, and sold.

production line factory system that allows parts to be added to an object as it is moved around

PROTECTION

There are no seat belts, bumpers, or airbags on a motorcycle. Riders must wear special clothing for protection.

HELMETS

The most popular type of helmet is "full-faced." It covers the whole head and has a flip-up **visor**. Special slots let air through to stop it from steaming up and getting hot. Riders of **vintage** bikes usually wear old-fashioned helmets to match. These are called "bash hats" or pilot helmets.

KEVLAR

Gloves are made from leather but the knuckles and wrists are strengthened by a tough material called Kevlar. The body armor areas in jackets, pants, and suits are also made from Kevlar.

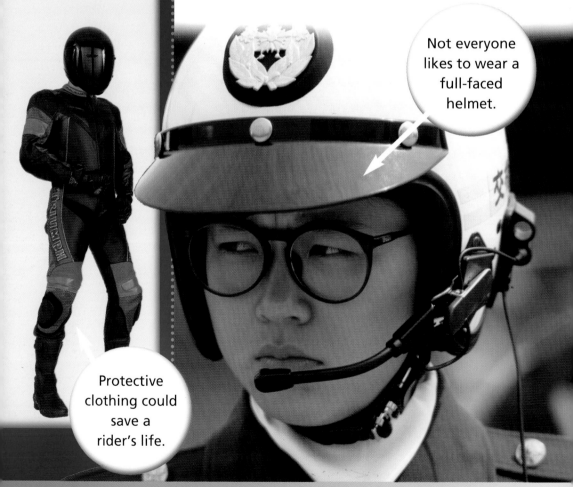

Not everyone likes to wear a full-faced helmet.

Protective clothing could save a rider's life.

BODY ARMOR

Jackets and pants often have thick pads on the knees, elbows, and shoulders. These pads are called body **armor**. They protect the body in an impact (see page 34).

LEATHER OUTFITS

Leather outfits can be worn as separate jackets and pants that are zipped together or as a one-piece racing suit. Motorcycle racers normally wear made-to-fit suits. Leather protects a rider's skin against "gravel rash." This is what happens if a rider falls and slides along the road.

BACK PROTECTOR

This is a hard pad worn against the back. It protects the backbone in an accident. Some leather outfits have a built-in back protector.

FOOTWEAR

Racing boots have thickly protected ankles. The toes and shins are protected by thick plastic. More casual-looking motorcycle boots also have this plastic protection sewn inside.

HELMET HELP

A helmet protects the rider in three ways:
1. The hard shell protects the head if it hits a hard object
2. The soft lining cushions the head in an impact
3. The shatter-proof visor protects the eyes.

This cutaway shows what is inside a helmet.

SOME DOS AND DON'TS

Do . . .

- wear the right protective clothing
- check the bike is safe each time you use it
- concentrate at all times.

Don't . . .

- pass or change direction without checking it is safe
- pass on a curve
- drive too close to other vehicles.

SPECIAL TRAINING

Motorcycle riders must be properly trained. On the roads, cars and trucks can be very dangerous to riders.

There are many things to learn, such as:
- the rules of the road
- handling the bike
- safety.

In some countries, new riders must attend training courses before they can practice on the road. In the United States, each state offers a similar course for free. They are taught by professional instructors. The first thing students learn is the layout of the bike and what all the controls do. Then they move on to basic riding, **gear changes,** and stopping the bike. Riders must be able to **accelerate** safely, stop quickly, and take corners smoothly.

Training courses teach new riders how to stay safe.

accelerate   go faster
gear change   changing the speed of an engine

DEVELOPING SKILLS

Next, riders develop their skills on **slalom courses**. These skills will help a rider in slow-moving traffic when they might have to turn sharply and quickly.

Riders learn how to do safe emergency stops and how to control skids. They learn how to spot problems with their machines and correct them.

Once riders are ready, they move on to public roads. They might have an instructor following them. New riders can then use the skills they have learned in real traffic. After this training, the rider is ready to take a test. If the rider passes, he or she is safe and skillful enough to feel confident and safe on the road.

RISKY LEFT TURNS

New riders should spend time practicing left turns. Without the proper training, these can be very dangerous. A left turn takes the rider across oncoming traffic. The rider could be hit by another vehicle.

Instructors teach new riders to see where the dangers are.

slalom course   traffic cones placed in a straight line, a few feet apart; riders weave in and out between them

MAKING MOTORCYCLES

Since the 1960s Japan has led the way in producing motorcycles. The Japanese have made more motorcycles than everyone else put together. The four big Japanese bike makers are Suzuki, Honda, Kawasaki, and Yamaha. They are sometimes called the Big Four.

TECH TALK

Suzuki GSX-R1000 K3: technical data
- Engine size: 988 cc
- Engine type: 4-cylinder
- Top speed: 175 mph (280 km/h)
- Weight: 370 lbs (168 kg)

This was voted International Bike of the Year in 2002.

THE BIG FOUR

The Big Four produce some of the best **performance** and **production motorcycles** on Earth. They **accelerate** incredibly quickly. They also have excellent **road-holding**.

The Kawasaki Ninja can reach a top speed of 182 mph (291 km/h).

frame   skeleton of bike that parts are added to
road-holding   ability of a vehicle to grip the road

THE HONDA FIREBLADE

The Honda Fireblade is a good example of the type of superbike made by the Big Four. This bike led to many great changes in bike design.

The Fireblade was first made in 1992. Many bikes have since copied features of its design. It started a **trend** away from huge engines. The Fireblade had a smaller engine than the superbikes made in the 1980s.

The Fireblade was much lighter than other bikes, so it did not have to be as powerful. It was the first of a new type of superbike. The light **frame** meant a sharper, quicker sports bike. Honda updates the Fireblade year after year, and it is still a best-seller.

TECH TALK

Honda CBR900RR Fireblade:
technical data
- Engine size: 954 cc
- Engine type: 4-cylinder in-line
- Engine power: 152 **bhp**
- Top speed: 169 mph (270 km/h)
- Weight: 370 lbs (168 kg)

A Honda Fireblade.

trend   popular taste at a given time

EUROPEAN BIKES

Japan may have the Big Four, but Europe also produces some very nice motorcycles. The main European bike makers include BMW, Ducati, Benelli, and Triumph.

Europe once had many other excellent motorbike makers, including BSA, Norton, Henderson, Scott, Velocette, and Sunbeam. Some of these have disappeared completely. Others only produce a small number of **custom** machines.

European bike makers now concentrate on producing **state-of-the-art** superbikes. A good example is the Benelli Novecento, below. Many experts think it is the best-looking **production motorcycle** ever made.

BMW K 1200GT

This BMW K 1200GT is almost as powerful as a top superbike. It also considers the passengers. It has many extras for comfort, such as a CD player, a radio between the rider and passenger, and even a heated seat.

A Benelli Novecento Tornado Tre 900.

custom   special or one-of-a-kind
radiator   part of an engine's cooling system

BEAUTIFUL BENELLI

The Novecento is unusual because the **radiator** is under the seat. This means the engine can be placed further forward, giving the bike excellent **stability**.

EUROPEAN COMPETITION

European bikes do not sell as well as Japanese bikes. They are well-known throughout the world, though. European bike makers tend to produce specialist bikes for serious motorcyclists.

European bikes also have a long history and tradition. Triumph and Ducati, for example, have been producing top-class superbikes for decades.

TRIUMPH DAYTONA

The original Triumph Daytona was popular in the 1960s. The modern version has state-of-the-art technology that makes it one of the most famous superbikes on the road today.

A Triumph Daytona 955i.

TECH TALK

Triumph Daytona 955i technical data

- Engine size: 956 **cc**
- Engine type: 3-**cylinders** in-line
- Engine power: 128 **bhp**
- Top speed: 157 mph (253 km/h)
- Weight: 494 lbs (224 kg)

stability   not likely to go wrong
state-of-the-art   using the latest technology

AMERICAN BIKES

Cruiser bikes are more about style and looking good than tearing around at high speeds. They are big, powerful, and comfortable to ride. The best-known maker of cruisers is the Wisconsin-based company Harley-Davidson.

The Harley-Davidson V-Rod mixes classic looks with **state-of-the-art** materials and technology.

V-ROD

The V-Rod's amazing design was inspired by Harley-Davidson's famous drag bikes. This bike appeals to those who love old-fashioned styling. People who prefer more modern looking motorcycles seem to like it, too.

HARLEY-DAVIDSON

Harley-Davidson make some of the most recognizable bikes. The Electra Glide Ultra Classic is perhaps the best known of all Harley-Davidson motorcycles. The first version hit the road in 1949. The design has been updated every few years ever since.

engineering   use of scientific techniques to improve production methods

ELECTRA GLIDE

The modern Electra Glide has a 1450 **cc** engine. The bike weighs 4,057 pounds (1,840 kilograms). It comes with a CD player and full sound system. You can even have speakers put into the rider's helmet or talk to a passenger on a radio.

Today's Harley-Davidson cruisers have all of the looks and styling of older motorcycles. They also have the **engineering** and technology of today's best bikes.

VICTORY VEGAS
The Victory Vegas is a modern version of a classic cruiser. It is powerful, very stylish and has lots of shiny chrome. Its 1500 cc engine is big enough to handle any hill.

The Harley-Davidson Electra Glide Ultra Classic has absolutely everything!

The Victory Vegas is a modern version of an old-style cruiser.

RACE ACTION

Giacomo Agostini, winner of 122 races.

Road or track racing bikes are designed for speed. The body is **streamlined,** and the tires are wide and smooth. The engines are ultra-powerful and **accelerate** very quickly.

THE RACING LINE

To win races riders look for the "racing line." This is the route that gets them around the track in the quickest time. Some races, such as the Isle of Man Tourist Trophy (TT) in Britian, are held on real roads. Other races, such as Grand Prix Championship races, are held on special tracks.

TT races on real roads were once part of the World Championship, but now they are separate events. They are more dangerous because they do not have the same safety features that tracks have.

The streamlined shape of a racing bike makes it go faster.

GIACOMO AGOSTINI

Giacomo Agostini won 122 races, more than anyone else. He won eight 500 cc and seven 350 cc World Championships. He also won ten Tourist Trophy titles. In the 1960s and 1970s he earned the nickname "swivel hips" because of his riding style.

streamlined shaped to cut through the air easily. This is important for fast bikes.

GRAND PRIX

The first Grand Prix took place in 1863. These races have been popular ever since. Hundreds of thousands of people come to watch a single race, with millions more watching on TV. Different classes of Grand Prix are run for different engine sizes. MotoGP, once known as the 500 cc Championship, is the most popular.

A different competition is "Superbike Racing." The bikes are very similar to bikes that are used on the road. Only small changes are allowed. This means the races are often close and exciting because the bikes are so similar.

FAMOUS RACERS

Track racers are the most famous motorcyclists. Racers like Barry Sheene, John Surtees, Mike Hailwood, and Carl Fogarty are known all over the world.

VALENTINO ROSSI

By the end of the 2003 season, Valentino Rossi had won 59 races and been world champion five times. At 25, he is the youngest rider to win all three of the 125 cc, 250 cc and 500 cc/MotoGP world titles.

Valentino Rossi holds the record for the most race points in a season.

RIDING STYLES

Fast bikes need special riding styles and techniques to make them go even faster.

The rider leans forward over the tank. This reduces the **air resistance**. The bike can cut through the air more easily.

Traveling in a straight line is simple. **Gravity** pulls the bike down and it is perfectly balanced. Cornering means that an outward **force** pulls on the bike and rider.

Riders have to be careful. If they lean over too far on a curve, they might fall off. Top racers have to judge corners correctly every single time. If they do not, the high speeds mean they will certainly fall off.

GEOFF DUKE

Riding styles have changed over the years. Geoff Duke was a huge star in the 1950s. He was World Champion six times. His riding style was very upright. He hardly ever moved his head. This is very different from the knee-down style of today.

Geoff Duke had a very different style from today's riders.

air resistance   slowing-down effect that air has against an object moving into it

LEANING IN

By leaning into turns, the weight of the bike and the rider acts against the outward force. Leaning over by the correct amount lowers the center of gravity. With the weight in the correct position, the machine goes quickly around the corner.

Riders also put one knee down towards the track to help this effect. The closer the weight is to the ground, the more **stable** the bike.

Tough pads protect the rider's knees.

Leaning over makes the bike turn faster around the corners.

LEANING FOR SAFETY

Leaning over so far in a corner looks really dangerous. However, riders are moving so fast that if they did not do this they would be in far more danger.

gravity   force that causes objects to fall toward the earth.

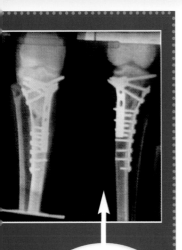

Barry Sheene's legs were shattered in racing accidents. This X-ray shows the metal pins holding his shin bones together.

BARRY SHEENE

Barry Sheene was World 500 **cc** Champion twice in the 1970s. He had two major crashes that almost killed him. His body was rebuilt using many steel plates, bolts, and pins. He became known as the "bionic man of motorsports."

ACCIDENTS

Bikes can be designed for safety and riders highly trained, but accidents will still happen. Mistakes on the road or track still cause injuries.

An accident on a bike is particularly dangerous. There are no seat belts or airbags to protect the rider. There is nothing at all between the rider and the road.

SLIDING

Sliding out is a common cause of accidents. This happens when a rider takes a corner too quickly or the road is slippery. The tires lose their grip and the bike slides to the outside of the curve. Sliding out happens often on race tracks.

SKIDS

Another common mistake is accelerating too quickly. This makes the rear wheel spin in one place. Braking too quickly can also cause a skid. Car drivers can usually stop their cars in a skid or a slide. Skidding or sliding on a bike is much worse because the rider will probably lose his or her balance and fall off.

BE SEEN AND BE SAFE

Accidents on the road often happen because motorcycles are difficult to see. They are much smaller than other vehicles on the road. If car drivers are not paying careful attention, they could miss a motorcyclist.

Bikers wear **reflective** clothing to make sure they are seen. Many motorcycles can only be ridden with the headlights on.

LEATHER

Leather is worn for two reasons. It provides good protection against scrapes and burns if a rider slides off their machine. It also gives the rider a **streamlined** shape, which makes the bike go faster.

Clothing is the only thing that protects riders in a crash.

TRACKS

Motocross tracks are often created using heavy, earth-moving machinery. The machines help make the dips, ramps, flat sections, and hills that the riders leap over. This is what makes the race exciting for riders and spectators.

MOTOCROSS

Motocross is off-road bike racing around specially created tracks. These tracks are full of obstacles, dangers, and high-speed sections.

TECHNIQUE

The riders use special techniques when they race. For most of the time, the rider does not sit on the seat. Standing up on the bike is called the "attack position." This is usually the best way to ride in motocross. Riders must be very skilled at jumps and landings.

About 40 riders compete in a race. They have to go around the track several times. The race lasts 30 to 40 minutes. Whoever gets around the course the fastest is the winner.

Motocross can be very exciting to watch.

THE BIKES

Motocross riders use special off-road bikes. They do not have a high top speed but they have great **acceleration**.

The bikes also have great **suspension** and **shock absorbers**. They need them to cope with all the jumps, bumps, and bangs. They also have knobby tires to help them grip the dirt. The brakes are sharp and powerful. **Gear changes** are lightning-fast. The engine and **exhaust pipe** are high up. This stops mud from getting clogged in them.

Motocross riders need to have great skill.

SAFETY

Because motocross is fast and dangerous, riders wear special clothing with lots of **armor** and padding. The riders must also be in good shape, strong, and have razor-sharp reactions.

TALK THE LANGUAGE

These terms are used to describe parts of a motocross track:

- **Berm:** banked-up corner
- **Drop off:** steep banks that must be jumped down
- **Tabletop:** jump with a flat top and a ramp at the end
- **Whoops:** bumpy section of track
- **Killer whoops:** very bumpy section of track.

shock absorbers part of a bike joined to the wheels that allow it to travel over bumps more smoothly

ENDURO EVENTS

An Enduro is a long-distance motorcycle race. Bikers race over difficult conditions and very rough terrain. The races are different lengths, but some are up to 1,000 miles (1,600 kilometers) long. There are also "Hare and Hounds" races, where riders complete as many laps as possible in a certain amount of time. Time can be very important in an Enduro race. Parts of the race are against the clock. But there are other parts where the challenge is just to finish!

Enduro is a popular sport. Thousands of riders take part in races all over the world. It is a true international sport.

The Baja 500 takes riders across about 500 miles (800 kilometers) of rough terrain.

Temperatures in the Sahara desert often reach 122°F (50°C).

BAJA 500

The Baja 500 is a popular desert Enduro. It starts and finishes in Ensenada, Mexico. The first race was in 1974. There are different races for different kinds of motorcycles.

ENDURO BIKES

The bikes used in Enduro are very similar to motocross bikes. They have lights, though, because some parts of an Enduro take place at night. They also have to be road legal, because some parts of the race might include normal roads.

PIT-STOPS

At the end of each race stage there are pit-stops where mechanics can check the bikes. The riders carry tents to sleep in at night.

THE BIG ONE

Paris to Dakar is probably the biggest Enduro race. It begins on Christmas Day (December 25) and lasts into January. The riders must cross the Sahara desert in 20 days. They ride more than 13,000 miles (21,000 kilometers).

AUSTRALIAN SAFARI

The Australian Safari is another very popular Enduro race. Bikers race across extreme desert conditions. The course changes each year.

The Australian Safari takes a different route across Australia each year.

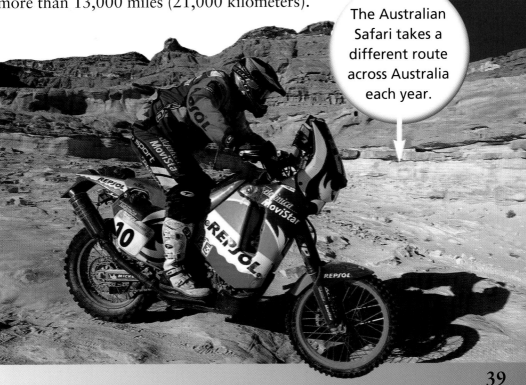

39

SPEEDWAY

Speedway is bike racing around small oval tracks. It started in the 1920s in Australia. It is fast, dangerous, and very exciting. It is now a popular sport all over the world.

Speedway bikes are unlike any other bikes you might see on the road. They are stripped down to the basics to keep them lightweight. The 500 **cc** bikes **accelerate** quickly. They can do 0-60 mph (0–96 km/h) in less than 3 seconds, which is as fast as a Formula One racing car. What makes it more dangerous is that the bikes have no brakes or gears to slow them down!

Ice speedway is popular in countries where winters are very cold.

Only the very brave and extremely skilled riders should try speedway racing.

ICE RACING

Ice racing is a type of speedway that is popular in Scandinavia and Eastern Europe. Riders make the most of the cold weather. The racing is similar to normal speedway, but without the dirt track. Instead, the bikes race on sheets of solid ice!

HOT HEATS

There are four riders in each race, two from each competing team. They ride 15 **heats**, with each heat being four laps of the track. The track is around 328 to 437 yards (300 to 400 meters) long but it is very narrow. The bikes shoot around the dirt track just inches away from each other. Any mistake and all the riders could have an accident.

The tracks are made from loosely packed gravel and dirt. This means the riders slide sideways around the curves, and accelerate along the short straightaway. The races are short, but very exciting. At the end of the heats, the team with the most points wins.

These spikes dig into the ice for better grip.

SPIKY TIRES

Ice-racing bikes have special tires to grip the ice. The tires have strong metal spikes. Unfortunately, the spikes are also very dangerous. If riders fall off their machines, they must be careful to avoid them.

TECH TALK

Other types of speedway racing:
- longtrack— much longer tracks, higher speeds, bigger bikes, two gears
- grasstrack— more riders in a race; many different types of races.

41

Without a wheelie bar, this bike would flip over.

DRAG-RACING

Drag-racing is the fastest sport on two wheels. Specially designed bikes are used that are incredibly powerful. They are designed to do one thing: **accelerate** in a straight line as fast as possible.

Drag bikes race in pairs over a track that is about 437 yards (400 meters) long. The race is over very quick because drag bikes reach 200 mph (320 km/h) in under 7 seconds. After the race it takes 875 yards to slow the bike down!

The rider lies flat over the fuel tank. This makes the machine more **streamlined**. It also helps to keep the front wheel down when accelerating.

DRAG ENGINES

The engine of a drag bike is so powerful it can lift the machine right off the ground. Wheelie bars are fixed to the back of the bike. They stop it from flipping over backwards.

Spinning the back wheel warms up the tire. A warm tire grips the track better.

UP TO SPEED   friction   force that slows things down when they move over each other and rub together

DRAG BIKE TIRES

The back tire of a drag bike is big and wide. The more rubber there is in contact with the track, the better grip the bike will have. Better grip means better acceleration.

Warm tires grip better than cold ones. Riders warm up tires before races by doing "burn-outs." They rev the engine with the front brake firmly on. The back tire spins and the **friction** between the tire and ground warms it up. This produces clouds of thick white smoke.

Repeated burn-outs mean the tires on a drag bike usually last for just six or seven races. Since races last for only a few seconds, the lifetime of a tire may be less than one minute!

A GSX 1588 dragster bike with wheelie bar attached.

GSX 1588 dragster: technical data
- Engine size: 1588 **cc**
- Engine type: 4-**cylinder** in-line
- Engine power: 375 **bhp**
- Top speed: 185 mph (296 km/h)
- Weight: 465 lbs (211 kg)
- Acceleration: 0–60 mph (0–100 km/h) in 1 second

Glenn Curtiss also designed and flew some of the earliest aircraft.

GLENN CURTISS

Glenn Curtiss became the fastest man alive in 1907. He rode a V8 bike across a Florida beach at 136 mph (218 km/h). He designed the bike himself, but his record is not officially recognized. This is because it was only over one run.

LAND-SPEED RECORD

There are many different types of **land-speed record**. Many riders try to break the land-speed record for motorcycles.

Most record attempts are made at the Bonneville Salt Flats in Utah. This is one of the only places that is long and flat enough for bikes to build up enough speed to break records.

To hold the official world record, two runs must be made inside a certain time. The **average** speed from the two runs is taken. This average speed is the one that ends up in the record books.

The Lightning Bolt broke the record in 1978.

average   mid-point between two or more numbers

LAND-SPEED RECORD HIGHLIGHTS: TWO WHEELS

Year	Rider	Bike	Average speed
1911	Jake de Rosier (USA)	Indian	85.4 mph (136.6 km/h)
1914	Sidney George (UK)	Indian	93.5 mph (149.6 km/h)
1920	Leslie Parkhurst (USA)	Harley-Davidson	103.8 mph (166 km/h)
1924	Herbert Le Vack (USA)	Brough Superior	118.9 mph (190.3 km/h)
1929	Ernst Henne (Germany)	BMW	134.7 mph (215.5 km/h)
1930	Joseph Wright (UK)	OEC-Temple	150.7 mph (241.2 km/h)
1937	Piero Taruff (Italy)	Gilera Rondine	170.4 mph (272.6 km/h)
1937	Ernst Henne (Germany)	BMW	174.4 mph (279 km/h)
1951	Willem Herz (Germany)	NSU Delphin	108.1 mph (288.2 km/h)
1955	Russell Wright (NZ)	Vincent Black Lightning	185.2 mph (296.2 km/h)
1962	William Johnson (USA)	Triumph Dudek	224.6 mph (359.3 km/h)
1970	Don Vesco (USA)	Yamaha	251.9 mph (403.1 km/h)
1975	Don Vesco (USA)	Yamaha Silver Bird	302.9 mph (484.7 km/h)
1978	Don Vesco (USA)	Kawasaki Lightning Bolt	318.6 mph (509.8 km/h)
1990	Dave Campos (USA)	Harley-Davidson	322.1 mph (515.4 km/h)

Ernst Henne rode a BMW each time he broke the speed record.

ERNST HENNE

Ernst Henne was a terrific speed rider, and the most successful. He broke the two-wheel land-speed record seven times. His first world record was in 1929, the last in 1937. His final record lasted for fourteen years.

land-speed record   fastest speed ever traveled by a particular type of vehicle

SPECIAL MOTORBIKES

Trailbiking is not a competitive sport. You do not earn points or ride against the clock. There is no competition involved. You just ride off-road in the country. Trailbiking is a great way to test your riding skills in difficult conditions.

It may not be a competition, but there are important trailbiking rules to follow. The main rule to remember is that bikers cannot simply ride their machines wherever they like. All land belongs to somebody, and bikers must have permission to ride there.

The engine of a trailbike is high off the ground to keep out mud.

Trailbikers ride off-road through all types of terrain.

RIDING HIGH

Trailbikes are similar to bikes used for motocross. Riders do not want mud to get trapped anywhere. This is why the mudguards, engine, and **exhaust pipe** are so high off the ground.

hazard danger

TAKING CARE

Bikers also need to remember that not everyone in the countryside likes motorcycles being there. It is important not to upset other people using the area. Careless riding could also cause damage to the environment.

The best idea is to join a club. These have regular meetings and help bikers to improve their riding skills. They give advice on the best places to train. They also organize events for members and get permission for the use of land.

TRIALS RIDING

Trials riding is the competition version of trailbiking. Riders have to get their machines over difficult **hazards** such as rocks or tree trunks. Speed is not as important in trials riding, but the riders' feet must not touch the ground.

Trials-riding courses are difficult and need skillful riding.

TECH TALK

REMEMBER
It is a criminal offense to ride a motorcycle:
- in public parks
- on the beach
- over farmland
- on sand dunes.

EMERGENCY!

Motorcycles are used all over the world by the **emergency services**. Police forces everywhere use them.

Some police forces use motorcycles because of their speed and power. Big bikes are able to catch up with most vehicles on the road. Another reason for using motorcycles is that they can get around quickly in cities and weave in and out of heavy traffic. A police motorcycle can sometimes get somewhere before a police car can. In some countries the police even use small scooters for this purpose.

All police bikes carry radio equipment and basic emergency supplies to help at an accident.

Police forces all over the world use motorcycles.

LAW ON TWO WHEELS

Many motorcycle makers produce bikes for the police. BMW make more than anyone else. It has produced more than 80,000 police bikes for use all over the world. Kawasaki, Harley-Davidson, and Honda also produce machines for the emergency services.

A California Highway Patrol rider.

emergency services   for example, medical services and police

CHiPS

The most famous police motorcycles are ridden by the California Highway Patrol (CHiPs for short). Their main task is to make sure that the law is followed on California's roads.

Until 1997 CHiPs rode Harley-Davidson and Kawasaki machines. Since then they have been changing over to BMWs. There are now almost 1000 BMW police motorcycles operating on California's highways.

helmet radio

warning lights

radio

PARAMEDIC

emergency equipment

Paramedics' bikes carry equipment for most emergencies.

TECH TALK

A popular TV show was made about the California Highway Patrol from 1977–1982. The show was called *CHiPs*. It was so popular that reruns are still being shown today.

AMBULANCE ACTION

In some large cities, ambulance staff use motorcycles. They carry most of the same equipment as a four-wheeled ambulance, but can get to the scene of an accident sooner. This is because they can dodge heavy traffic.

EDDIE KIDD

Eddie Kidd made more than 12,000 jumps without breaking a bone. He jumped the Great Wall of China and fourteen double-decker buses. But in 1996 he was badly injured in a crash that ended his career.

Eddie Kidd jumps over a line of buses.

STUNT RIDING

Stunt riding is for people who are very skilled and more than a little crazy! They attempt amazing tricks and dangerous jumps. It takes great nerve and skill to be a stunt rider.

Stunt riders jump over rows of cars or across canyons. They ride through flames and along tightropes.

Evel Knievel's "skycycle."

Some even jump off their bikes and "ski" along behind by holding on to the **frame** at over 100 mph (160 km/h)!

Doing a "wheelie" is riding just on the back wheel. One stunt rider has done a wheelie at 192 mph (307 km/h). Another rider did a 145-mile (232-kilometer) long wheelie!

EVEL KNIEVEL

Evel Knievel is the world's most famous stunt rider. He made many famous jumps in the 1970s and had several accidents. Knievel joked that he had broken every bone in his body.

In 1974 he tried to jump 1,640 feet (500 meters) over Snake River Canyon in Idaho. He used a specially designed "skycycle" powered by rockets, pictured left. Evel made it across the canyon but the skycycle's parachute opened too early. Strong winds blew him back. He floated down and landed just a few feet from the river, where he probably would have drowned.

Evel's son, Robbie, carries on in his father's footsteps. In 1999 he jumped 230 feet (70 meters) over the Grand Canyon.

POLICE STUNTS

Because the police use motorcycles, some have their own display teams. They can do stunts that include jumping over obstacles and riding through fire.

This pyramid involves fifteen policemen.

One of the latest custom-painted helmets by Richard Stevens.

CUSTOM BIKES

A **custom** bike can be many things. It might be a **mass-produced** machine that has been altered in some way. It might be given a paint-job or have a **highly-tuned** engine put in. It may even be a one-of-a-kind special made from scratch.

Whatever the case, custom bikes are special. They look different from everything else. People who make or buy custom bikes want to own something that no one else has—anywhere!

Custom bikes often have unusual and spectacular paint-jobs. Sometimes even the engine parts are painted. Special paint designs are often done by professional artists and can cost a lot of money.

Some people want their bike to be unique, or the only one of its kind.

CUSTOMIZED HELMETS

Custom designs can go beyond the machine itself. Some riders even have designs painted on their helmets to match the bike they are riding.

highly tuned   adjusted to make more powerful
mass-produced   made in large numbers

SPECIAL TECHNOLOGY

Other custom bikes are designed for technology rather than good looks. Some may have special lightweight **frames** that make them super-quick. Others may have special engines or improved **suspension**.

SHOWING OFF

Owners of custom bikes sometimes take them to custom competition shows. These shows are held all over the world. They give the public a chance to see hundreds of amazing motorcycles in the same place. Judges award prizes to the best-looking bikes.

Some custom bikes are very valuable. This is because the parts are specially made. Sometimes parts are even made out of precious materials such as gold.

TRIKES

Some custom machines even have an extra wheel. They are called **trikes.** They are quite rare and have to be specially built.

A customized trike.

trike motorbike with three wheels

SCOOTERS

Scooters are small and light. They do not **perform** or handle as well as motorcycles, but they are still a lot fun to ride.

Scooters have come in and out of fashion over the years. In the 1960s they were very popular in Europe. All of the **mods** had to have one with as many lights and mirrors as possible.

This Honda Silver Wing scooter looks more like a motorcycle.

In recent years the scooter has become popular again, especially in cities. Scooters can get around quickly in traffic jams. They use little fuel, so they are cheap to run.

THE HONDA SILVER WING

The Honda Silver Wing is one of the most powerful scooters. It has many luxury features built in and looks like some of the larger cruising motorcycles.

The BMW C1 has many built-in safety features.

mod   in the 1960s one of a group of people who liked the same music, wore stylish clothing, and rode scooters

SCOOTER WITH A ROOF!

The BMW C1, pictured on page 54, is the first scooter to have a roof. The rider sits inside a strong steel **frame**. So this scooter is safer than most two-wheeled machines. The steel frame protects the rider in an accident.

The C1 has all the advantages of a scooter around a city, but it also has added safety. It even comes with seat belts.

The C1 also has another advantage. It is the only two-wheeled vehicle that keeps the rider dry in the rain!

TECH TALK

In many countries and states you do not have to wear a helmet when riding a scooter. But smart riders always wear a helmet to stay safe.

PEUGEOT SPEEDFIGHT

The Peugeot Speedfight is one of the world's best-selling scooters. It has classic styling but the technology is **state-of-the-art**. It has either a 50 **cc** or 100 cc engine and is very light.

The Peugeot Speedfight is a popular modern design.

BIKES OF THE FUTURE

Some future bikes are just too amazing for words. The Tomahawk was an experiment that got lots of publicity. It may even go on sale one day, but there are no plans at present. Only the very rich would be able to buy one. The bike needs four wheels to handle the power of the huge engine. Each pair of wheels is very close together.

The engine of the Tomahawk is bigger than most Porsche and Ferrari engines. Some military tanks have smaller engines!

A KTM diesel bike.

DIESEL BIKES

Another challenge for designers is to produce a diesel engine that is powerful, but small enough to fit inside a standard frame.

The Dodge Tomahawk may become a reality one day.

TECH TALK

Dodge Tomahawk concept: technical data
- Engine and size—Viper V10, 8277 **cc**
- Engine power: 500 **bhp**
- Top speed (untested)— 400 mph (640 km/h)
- Weight: 1,504 lbs (682 kg)
- Acceleration: 0-60 mph (0–96 km/h) in 2.5 seconds

carbon-fiber   very hard, strong, light material

NEW MATERIALS

Motorcycle design is improving all the time. Bikes are becoming lighter as new materials are used. Aluminum and **carbon-fiber frames** make bikes very light. The less they weigh, the less power they need to move them. This uses less fuel, which is better for the environment.

Computers produce impressive **streamlined** designs. Designers are also working hard to make fuel more efficient. The bikes of the future should be faster, lighter, and have better handling.

What they will look like is hard to say. We often imagine that machines in the future will be unlike anything around today. Many bikes of the future could be based on past designs, however. This is called retro-styling.

NEW FUEL

Designers have known for years that gasoline engines are not the most efficient. They are working hard to find different power sources for motorcycles. Other possibilities include electricity or hydrogen. Bikers of the future may plug their motorcycles in to recharge rather than go to a gas station.

This was the first London taxi to be powered by a hydrogen fuel cell.

MOTORCYCLE FACTS

Manufacturers with the most Moto GP wins		
Manufacturer	**First win**	**Wins to end 2002**
Honda	1961	536
Yamaha	1963	401
MV Agusta	1952	275
Suzuki	1962	153
Aprilia	1987	140
Kawasaki	1969	85
Derbi	1970	81
Kreidler	1962	65
Garelli	1982	51
Gilera	1949	47

The world's longest motorcycle jump is 253 feet (77 meters).

There is a river in Arkansas named after Evel Kneivel, the motorcycle daredevil.

On August 2, 2003, Billy Baxter rode a Kawasaki Ninja ZX-12R at 165 mph (265 km/h) along a runway in Wiltshire, England. Billy Baxter is blind.

The world's highest motorcycle jump is 55 feet (17 meters).

Riders with the most Moto GP Wins		
Rider	**Years**	**Wins**
Giacomo Agostini	1965–76	122
Angel Nieto	1969–85	90
Mike Hailwood	1959–67	76
Valentino Rossi	1996–2003	59
Rolf Biland	1975–90	56
Mick Doohan	1990–98	54
Phil Read	1961–75	52
Jim Redman	1961–66	45
Anton Mang	1976–88	42
Carlo Ubbiali	1950–60	39

The world's tallest rideable motorcycle is *Bigtoe*, which has a height of 14 feet (4.3 meters) and a top speed of 62 mph (100 km/h). It is powered by a Jaguar V12 engine. The bike cost $80,000 to build.

The world's longest motorcycle is 25 feet (7.5 meters) long. It weighs nearly 4,409 pounds (1,999 kilograms). The monster machine was designed and built in Australia. The bike, named *Big Ben*, has a set of training wheels to keep it upright while still. During a test drive, *Big Ben* achieved a speed of 110 mph (177 km/h).

FIND OUT MORE

BOOKS

Freeman, Gary. *Motocross*. Chicago: Heinemann
  Library, 2002.
Graham, Ian. *Superbikes*. Chicago: Heinemann
  Library, 2003.
Henshaw, Peter. *The Encyclopedia of Motorcycles*.
  Broomall, Penn: Chelsea House, 2000.

WORLD WIDE WEB

If you want to find out more, you can search the
Internet using keywords like these:
superbikes + fastest
"Valentino Rossi"
Motocross
Harley-Davidson

Make your own keywords using headings or
words from this book. Using the search tips
opposite will help you to find the most useful
websites.

WEB SITES

**MOTORCYCLE
SAFETY
FOUNDATION (MSF)**
Information on
how to stay safe.
Also shows where
to go in your area
to sign up for a
training class.
msf-usa.org

SEARCH TIPS

There are billions of pages on the Internet so it can be difficult to find exactly what you are looking for. If you just type in "motorcycle" on a search engine like Google, you will get a list of millions web pages. These search skills will help you find useful websites more quickly:

- Use simple keywords, not whole sentences
- Use two to six keywords in a search
- Be precise. Only use names of people, places, or things
- If you want to find words that go together, put quote marks around them, for example "world-speed record"
- Use the advanced section of your search engine
- Use the + sign between keywords to find pages with all these words.

WHERE TO SEARCH

SEARCH ENGINE

A search engine looks through the entire web and lists all sites that match the search words. The best matches are at the top of the list, on the first page. Try **google.com**

SEARCH DIRECTORY

A search directory is like a library of websites. You can search by keyword or subject and browse through the different sites like you look through books on a library shelf. A good example is **yahooligans.com**

GLOSSARY

accelerate go faster

acceleration how quickly something speeds up

air resistance slowing-down effect that air has against an object moving into it

armor protective covering

automatically on its own, without a person working it

average mid-point between two or more numbers

bhp rate at which an engine does work

bonding joining

carbon fiber very hard, strong, light material

cc (cubic centimeters) this number measures the size of an engine's cylinders. A higher number means a larger engine.

component single part from something larger

crankshaft part of an engine that is joined to the pistons

cruiser motorcycle built for comfort, looks, and style rather than performance

custom special or one-off

cylinder tube-shaped part of an engine where fuel is burned

emergency services for example, medical services and police

engineering use of scientific techniques to improve production methods

exhaust pipe that lets out smoke and fumes

force push or a pull

four-stroke engine where each piston moves up and down four times after each spark of the engine

frame skeleton of the bike that the other parts are added to

friction force that slows things down when they move over each other and rub together

gear change changing the speed of an engine

golden age great period in a history

gravity force that causes objects to fall toward the Earth

hazard danger

heat part of a race

highly tuned adjusted to make more powerful

integral parts parts of a bike built in a single piece, instead of joining several pieces together

land-speed record fastest speed ever traveled by a particular type of vehicle

limited edition when only a small number are built

mass-produced made in large numbers

military to do with the armed forces, especially the army

mod in the 1960s one of a group of people who liked the same music, wore stylish clothing, and rode scooters

perform / performance how well a bike does things

piston disk or cylinder that moves up and down inside a tube

production line factory system that allows parts to be added to an object as it is moved around

production motorcycles bikes that are built in large numbers to be bought by the public

radiator part of an engine's cooling system

reflective throws off light

reputation being well known for something

road-holding ability of a vehicle to grip the road

shock absorber part of a bike joined to the wheels that allow it to travel over bumps more smoothly

sidecar small car attached to the side of a motorcycle

slalom course traffic cones placed in a straight line a few feet apart. Riders must weave in and out between them.

spark plug part of an engine that makes an electrical spark

spoke metal rod that runs from the center of a wheel to the outside edge

stable / stability not likely to go wrong

state-of-the-art using the latest technology

streamlined shaped to cut easily through the air. This is very important for fast bikes

stunt dangerous trick

suspension part of a bike that joins the wheels to the frame. It contains springs that allow the bike to pass over bumps more easily

transmitted passed from one place to another

trend popular taste at a given time

trike motorbike with three wheels

two-stroke engine where each piston moves up and down twice after each spark of the engine

vibration very rapid shaking

vintage old, usually built between 1919 and 1930

visor see-through part of a helmet that can normally be raised up

welding way of joining metals by melting them together

Raintree would like to thank the following for information used in the book:
The Top Ten of Everything 2004, Dorling Kindersley, 2003.